THE ROOSTER'S ANTLERS

A Story of the Chinese Zodiac

retold by Eric A. Kimmel • illustrated by YongSheng Xuan

Holiday House / New York

L ONG AGO, when the world was new, the Jade Emperor
created a calendar to measure time. He said, "I will name each
of the twelve years in my calendar after an animal. The wisest,
the bravest, the swiftest, the most beautiful animals will be chosen."

The animals were very excited. Whom would the Jade Emperor choose? Everyone was sure Rooster would be picked. He had colorful feathers, a bright red comb, and a glorious pair of coral antlers. "I am the most beautiful animal of all!" he crowed. "The Jade Emperor has to choose me."

Dragon was also a splendid creature, but he was much less certain that he would be chosen. Dragon had a bald head and was very sensitive about it. "I wish I could do something about my head," Dragon complained to his friend Centipede. "Nobody ever looks at my colorful scales, my rippling mane, or my magnificent tail. They just stare at my head. If I had antlers like Rooster, no one would notice that my head is bald."

Centipede was a sly, wormlike creature, without the many legs and stinging jaws he has today. He was always scheming and telling lies about the other animals. His only friend was Dragon, who felt sorry for him. "What would you give me if I got Rooster's antlers for you?" Centipede asked Dragon.

"I'd give you many legs and powerful jaws," Dragon said. "You wouldn't need me to protect you. You could defend yourself."

"Good!" Centipede exclaimed. "I'd be fierce and powerful. All the other animals would be afraid of me. They'd have to do whatever I told them, whether they liked it or not. Don't worry, Dragon. I'll make sure the Jade Emperor picks you. You'll be wearing Rooster's antlers."

Centipede crawled away to visit Rooster.

"What do you want, Centipede?" Rooster snapped.

"Dragon needs a favor," Centipede whined. "You know how ashamed he is about his bald head. He is embarrassed to let the Jade Emperor see him. But if he were wearing your beautiful antlers . . ."

". . . no one would notice that he is bald. So Dragon wants to borrow my antlers. Very well, he can have them." Rooster had a generous nature. He also knew he was certain to be chosen by the Jade Emperor, with or without antlers.

"Dragon can keep my antlers as long as he needs them," said Rooster. He assumed Dragon would send them back after the Jade Emperor made his choice.

Centipede grinned as he took the antlers from Rooster. These were exactly the words he wanted to hear. "Thank you, Rooster. Dragon will be so grateful."

Centipede hurried back to Dragon. "Here are Rooster's antlers!" Centipede told him. "He says you may keep them as long as you need them."

"Rooster is very kind. And you are very clever to get me his beautiful coral antlers," Dragon replied as he fitted the antlers onto his head. He looked at himself in the mirror. "How splendid I am! No one will notice my bald head now!" He turned to Centipede. "I will give you what I promised. Crawl into my magic jar."

Centipede crawled into Dragon's magic jar. Dragon filled the jar with earth, air, fire, and water. He sprinkled it with golden scales from his tail, then waved it toward the four directions: north, south, east, and west.

Dragon banged a gong. "Come out, Centipede!"

When Centipede emerged from the jar, he was a different creature. He no longer crawled on his belly; he had many legs to carry him. He no longer wheedled and whined; his mouth held powerful stinging jaws. Centipede ran around in circles, exercising his new legs, snapping his jaws at passing flies.

"Thank you, Dragon! Now I am fierce and powerful. All other animals will tremble before me!"

"Don't brag, Centipede," Dragon cautioned him. "Even when one is mighty, it is still important to speak softly and act modestly. Besides, you may not be as mighty as you think."

Soon afterward, the Jade Emperor summoned the animals to his palace. As Rooster preened and strutted before the mirrors, he noticed Dragon wearing his antlers.

"How splendid you look!" Rooster said politely.

"Thank you," Dragon replied. "It's the antlers."

I know, thought Rooster. *I made a big mistake. I should have kept those antlers for myself.*

The Jade Emperor looked at all the animals. Finally he announced his choices. Rat was chosen for his cleverness; Ox for his strength; Tiger for her fierceness; Rabbit for her gentleness; Dragon for his wisdom; Snake for her cunning; Horse for his swiftness; Ram for his courage; Monkey for her intelligence; Rooster for his beauty; Dog for her loyalty; and Pig for his good nature and common sense.

"The Twelve Earthly Branches of the cycle of the years will be named after these noble animals. Their portraits will be placed in heaven, to shine forever among the stars."

The chosen animals congratulated one another. All were pleased to be honored. All except Rooster.

"What? Dragon was the fifth chosen and I was only tenth! If I hadn't given away my antlers, I would have been fifth, instead of Dragon. No! I would have been first, instead of Rat. Why was I so stupid? Why did I let Centipede talk me into lending my antlers?"

Rooster stormed up to Dragon. "Give back my antlers!" he demanded.

"I will not," said Dragon. "You told Centipede I could keep your antlers for as long as I needed them. Well, I'm still bald, so I still need them. I promise to give them back if I ever grow hair. Unfortunately, it may be a while. No dragon has grown hair on top of his head for ten thousand years."

"You cheated me! You're as bad as Centipede!" Rooster screamed. But Dragon just smiled as he floated away among the clouds.

Rooster marched home, ruffling his feathers, upset and angry. Along the way he met Centipede.

"It's your fault that Dragon stole my antlers! You tricked me!"

"Not so!" Centipede replied. "You're the one who said Dragon could keep them as long as he needed to. If you don't like it, too bad!"

Rooster squawked with rage. He flew at Centipede. But Centipede did not run away. Instead, he charged back and forth, snapping his jaws.

"Beware, Rooster! I'm not afraid of you. I have many, many legs. I have strong stinging jaws. I can tear you apart. There won't be a feather left of you when I'm done."

"Why, you arrogant little worm!" Rooster crowed. "First you steal my antlers. Now you threaten me!"

Centipede should have remembered Dragon's words of warning. He was not nearly as ferocious as he thought. His legs could not carry him as fast as Rooster could fly. Nor could his stinging jaws hurt Rooster's beak. Rooster chased him back and forth, clawing and pecking him mercilessly. Centipede barely escaped with his life. He crawled under a rock. Here he waited in terrified silence until Rooster went away.

Rooster and his descendants have hated centipedes since that day. They blame them for the loss of their antlers. Whenever Rooster spies a centipede scurrying around the barnyard, he gobbles him up.

Rooster still hopes to recover his antlers. He can often be seen perched on a fence, flapping his wings, stretching out his neck, and crowing in his loudest voice,

"Ku-keri-keru! Dragon, you thief! Give back my antlers!"

But Dragon, floating high above the clouds, only smiles and pretends he doesn't hear.

Chinese Zodiac Animals

RATS are clever and ambitious. Success comes easily to them. They do not fear hard work, but have little patience with those who are less motivated. Dragons and monkeys make good partners for rats. Not horses!

OXEN are strong, steady, and well-liked, although some find them boring and unimaginative. Oxen enjoy the company of snakes and roosters. They should avoid rams.

TIGERS are heroes. Fiercely loyal to their friends, they never turn away from a fight. Tigers will attempt impossible tasks and will often succeed due to their courage, cunning, and aggressiveness. Horses and dogs make good companions for tigers. Monkeys do not.

RABBITS have loving, sensitive natures. They want everyone to be friends. Rabbits make good counselors and peacemakers, but they often have difficulty standing up for themselves and worry too much about what others think. Rabbits enjoy the company of rams and pigs. They don't get along with roosters.

DRAGONS appear terrifying at first, but those who take the time to know them quickly learn that they are wise, energetic, and imaginative. Dragons inspire others with their own enthusiasm, which makes them natural leaders. They do not do well in situations where they have to share power or consult with others. Monkeys and rats enjoy being on dragon's team. Dogs do not.

SNAKES say little and do much. They pursue their goals with quiet intensity, never giving up until they achieve success. Snakes prefer to work alone. If they must have partners, it is best to choose roosters or oxen. Never pigs.

HORSES are friendly and well-liked, although they can lose their tempers when they don't get their way. They get along best with dogs and tigers. Rats should be avoided.

RAMS are brave, creative, and have a fine sense of style. They may become fearful when they feel unsure of themselves. Rabbits and pigs make good friends. Rams tend to butt heads with oxen.

MONKEYS are exceptionally clever and persuasive. They excel at bringing others around to their point-of-view, but tend to give up too quickly if they don't succeed right away. Monkeys enjoy the company of dragons and rats. They do not get along with tigers.

ROOSTERS are perfectionists. They drive themselves to succeed, but at the price of paying too little attention to the feelings of those around them. That is why Roosters are regarded as odd or self-centered. Snakes and oxen understand them. Rabbits do not.

DOGS are brave, honest, and generous with their time and talents. Others look up to them. They tend to be stubborn. Dogs have difficulty adjusting to change. They get along best with horses and tigers. Dragons mean trouble.

PIGS are kind and good-hearted. Nonetheless, they often act without thinking and get angry when events don't work out as they hoped. Pigs make friends easily with rams and rabbits, but not with snakes.

Text copyright © 1999 by Eric A. Kimmel
Illustrations copyright © 1999 by YongSheng Xuan
All Rights Reserved
Printed in the United States of America
First Edition

Typography by Lynn Braswell

Library of Congress Cataloging-in-Publication Data
Kimmel, Eric A.
The rooster's antlers: a story of the Chinese zodiac/retold by Eric A. Kimmel;
illustrated by YongSheng Xuan.
p. cm.
Summary: Relates how the Jade Emperor chose twelve animals to represent the years in his calendar.
Also discusses the Chinese calendar, zodiac, the qualities associated with each animal,
and what animal rules the year in which the reader was born.
ISBN 0–8234–1385–3
[1. Zodiac—Folklore. 2. Animals—Folklore. 3. Folklore—China. 4. Astrology, Chinese.]
I. Xuan, YongSheng, ill. II. Title.
PZ8.1.K567Ro 1999 398.2'0951'0452—dc21
[E] 97–46854 CIP AC

Author's Note

The Chinese calendar has been in use for thousands of years. The year begins on the second new moon after the winter solstice, which makes it fall between January 21 and February 19 on the Western calendar. The years are grouped into 12-year cycles. Each year in the cycle is named after one of the 12 animals of the Chinese zodiac. Sixty years, five of these 12-year cycles, makes up a complete cycle.

An excellent book about the festivals and celebrations of the Chinese year is *Mooncakes and Hungry Ghosts* by Carol Stephanchuk and Charles Wong.

I learned the story of *The Rooster's Antlers* the traditional way, hearing it told by another teller when I was in junior high school. The teller was Mr. Sam Lum, who had a store in our neighborhood. Mr. Lum was from Hong Kong. He told us many stories from China. I liked this one best, because my dad, like Dragon, had a bald head. There aren't many stories about bald-headed people, which may explain why I thought this one was so funny. I still feel that way, even though I, like Dragon, now have my own bald head.